smoothies and juices

NUTRITIOUS AND DELICIOUS DRINKS
FOR EVERY OCCASION

CHRISTINE AMBRIDGE
MAIN PHOTOGRAPHY BY CALVEY TAYLOR–HAW

p

This is a Parragon Publishing Book
This edition published in 2004

Parragon Publishing
Queen Street House
4 Queen Street
Bath BA1 1HE, UK

Created and produced for Parragon by The Bridgewater Book Company Ltd.

Home economist Michaela Jester

ISBN: 1-40540-630-5

Printed in China

NOTE

*This book uses imperial and metric measurements. Follow the same units of
measurement throughout; do not mix imperial and metric. All spoon measurements
are level: teaspoons are assumed to be 5 ml and tablespoons are assumed to be 15 ml.
Unless otherwise stated, milk is assumed to be whole milk, eggs and individual vegetables
such as potatoes are medium, and pepper is freshly ground black pepper.*

*The times given for each recipe are an approximate guide only because the preparation
times may differ according to the techniques used by different people and they include chilling and
marinating times, where appropriate.*

*Recipes using raw or very lightly cooked eggs should be avoided by infants, the elderly,
pregnant women, convalescents, and anyone suffering from an illness.*

Contents

Introduction

It is no surprise that smoothies and mixed juices have become so fashionable in these health-conscious days. Commercial soft drinks and even some fruit juices often contain ingredients that many of us would rather avoid—artificial colorings and flavorings, high levels of sugar or chemical sweeteners, and preservatives. In addition, many of them are so sickly, bland,

Nutritionists recommend that we should eat at least five portions of fruit and vegetables a day. Modern life is so busy, however, that few of us have the time or inclination to plan, shop, prepare, and cook balanced meals every day of the week. The good news is that in the few minutes it takes to juice a handful of carrots and tomatoes, or to whizz some berries and yogurt in the food

or unexciting that they simply do not appeal to the adult palate. Making fruit and vegetable drinks at home ensures that we know precisely what they contain. It also means that we can mix them to taste truly delicious. What is more, we can guarantee that the raw ingredients are organic, if that's what we want.

processor, we can produce the equivalent of one of those portions. Better still, the ingredients are usually raw and the juice or smoothie will be consumed immediately. So there is less possibility of nutrients leaching out during cooking or being destroyed through excessive exposure to air. This makes the drink even healthier.

You can make smoothies and juices from most fruit and vegetables. The golden rule is never to combine the two, with the exceptions of apples and carrots which go with just about everything, and tomatoes, a fruit that most treat as a vegetable. The recipes in this book will give you an excellent starting point, and should provide you with lots of ideas for inventing your own drinks. Generally, once people have begun the habit of making their own fruit and vegetable drinks, they become great enthusiasts and never feel the need to return to commercial brands.

Of course, smoothies and juices are enjoyable thirst quenchers, but there is much more to them than this. Many provide a powerful boost that can kick-start the day at breakfast time or revive flagging energy in the afternoon, with a healthy nutritional balance that you won't find in a packet of cookies or a chocolate bar. Apples, for example, are a powerhouse of slow-release carbohydrate, the kind that keeps you going for several hours. Citrus fruits, berries, and, above all, kiwi fruit are packed with vitamin C;

strawberries and raspberries contain iron; and carrots are a valuable source of beta-carotene. In addition, with a juicer (see page 6), some of the fiber is incorporated in the drink and not discarded.

The recipes in this book are divided into three chapters—Fruits, Vegetables & Spices, and Sweets & Coffees. The selection of delicious drinks does not only include smoothies and mixed juices, but also coolers and other long drinks; pick-me-ups; tea- and coffee-based mixes; and some lovely milkshakes for a special treat. You will also find some useful information about equipment and ways of preparing ingredients to set you on the right path to complete success in making your own healthy and tasty fruit and vegetable concoctions.

Essentials

Making smoothies and juices is great fun, as well as being very healthy. All you need are the right ingredients and equipment, some recipes, and your imagination.

You don't have to spend a lot of money on equipment, but for the best and freshest results, you will need a food processor and a juicer.

A basic kitchen food processor with a standard metal blade mixes smoothies to perfection in a few moments, and the recipes in this book assume that one will be used. You might also be able to use a blender, depending on how robust the model is. However, unless your food processor has a juicer attachment, you cannot use it for making juice, as it will just turn the ingredients into a purée. A juicer, on the other hand, separates the pulp from the juice.

There are three types of juicer, and these vary considerably in price. Centrifugal juicers are at the lower end of the price range. Coarsely chopped ingredients are fed into this type of machine, which grates them into tiny pieces and spins them at high speed. The liquid is extracted by centrifugal force, leaving the fruit or vegetable pulp behind. As the fruit and vegetables are exposed to the air throughout the process, juices made by this method are thought to have the lowest nutritional content.

Hydraulic juicers are at the top end of the price range. Extreme pressure forces the juice out of the ingredients, through a strainer and into a pitcher, leaving the pulp behind. Juices pressed by this method are very high in nutrients.

The third type, triturating juicers, are in the middle of the price range and the juice they produce is in the middle of the nutritional range. A rotating cutter tears up the ingredients and simultaneously presses them against a strainer.

Besides cost, other aspects to consider before buying a juicer are size—triturating juicers tend to be larger than the others—the speed at which they work, and how easy they are to clean. But whichever type of juicer you choose, you can still be sure that the drink you are creating will be full of nutrients as well as flavor.

Any other equipment you are likely to need, from a chopping board to an ice-cube tray, you will almost certainly already have in your kitchen cupboards.

Techniques

When you use a food processor, everything that goes into the goblet will be incorporated into the final drink. Consequently, fruit and vegetables must be washed, peeled, and prepared in the same way as for any other type of recipe. Pits, pips, and seeds must all be removed. Large, firm fruit and vegetables, such as apples and carrots, should be coarsely chopped before being placed in the processor.

If you are going to add ice cubes to the food processor, crush them first. You can do this by wrapping the ice cubes in a clean tea towel and hammering them with a meat mallet or the side of a rolling pin.

The technique with juicers, whatever type you are using, is different because the juice and solid residue are kept separate. Most vegetables and fruits, with the obvious exceptions of bananas, kiwi fruit and citrus fruits, do not need to be peeled. However, it is still important that they are thoroughly washed.

Some juicers can cope with quite tough skins, even including the skins of melons. Many of the nutrients in fruits lie just below the surface of the skin, so this is a particularly valuable asset, but it does mean that you must be sure to use specimens with undamaged skin.

As a rough guide to making your own fresh juices, 1 lb 2 oz/500 g of raw carrots or apples yields 8 fl oz/225 ml of juice while 1 lb 2 oz/500 g of tomatoes or blackberries will produce 325 ml/11 fl oz of fresh juice.

You can leave vegetable tops, such as beet leaves, attached, but do trim off the roots. Coarse outer leaves that would be removed for other culinary purposes don't need trimming. Pits, such as those in cherries, peaches, and mangoes, should be removed, but you can leave smaller seeds and pips in grapes, apples, and pears. Then the process of actually making the juice is very simple.

Fruits

Melon Medley

This summer smoothie, with three different kinds of melon, is deliciously refreshing on a hot day.

serves 2

1 cup natural yogurt

¾ cup honeydew melon, roughly chopped

¾ cup cantaloupe melon, roughly chopped

¾ cup watermelon, roughly chopped

6 ice cubes

wedges of melon, to decorate

Method

❶ Pour the yogurt into a food processor. Add the honeydew melon pieces and process until smooth.

❷ Add the cantaloupe and watermelon pieces along with the ice cubes and process until smooth. Pour the mixture into glasses and decorate with wedges of melon. Serve at once.

Nectarine Melt

Mango and nectarine is an inspired combination, made all the more special with
the clever addition of lemon sorbet.

serves 2

1 cup milk	1 ripe mango, pitted and diced
2 cups lemon sorbet	2 ripe nectarines, pitted and diced

Method

❶ Pour the milk into a food processor, add half of the lemon sorbet, and process gently until combined. Add the remaining sorbet and process until smooth.

❷ When the mixture is thoroughly blended, gradually add the mango and nectarines and process until smooth. Pour the mixture into glasses, add straws, and serve.

Orange & Lime Iced Tea

Sweet and sharp citrus flavors turn a very simple drink into a subtle and sophisticated thirst quencher.

serves 2

1¼ cups water	To decorate
2 tea bags	wedge of lime
scant ½ cup orange juice	sugar
4 tbsp lime juice	slices of fresh orange, lemon, or lime
1–2 tbsp brown sugar	
8 ice cubes	

Method

❶ Pour the water into a pan and bring to a boil. Remove from the heat, add the tea bags, and leave to infuse for 5 minutes. Remove the tea bags and leave the tea to cool to room temperature (about 30 minutes). Transfer to a pitcher, cover with plastic wrap, and chill in the refrigerator for at least 45 minutes.

❷ When the tea has chilled, pour in the orange juice and lime juice. Add sugar to taste.

❸ Take two glasses and rub the rims with a wedge of lime, then dip them in sugar to frost. Put the ice cubes into the glasses and pour over the tea. Decorate the rims with slices of fresh orange, lemon, or lime and serve.

Fruit Cooler

Power up with breakfast in a glass, packed with protein, vitamins, and slow-release carbohydrate—and a sensational flavor, too.

serves 2

1 cup orange juice

½ cup natural yogurt

2 eggs

2 bananas, sliced and frozen

slices of fresh banana, to decorate

Method

❶ Pour the orange juice and yogurt into a food processor and process gently until combined.

❷ Add the eggs and frozen banana slices and process until smooth. Pour the mixture into glasses and decorate the rims with slices of fresh banana. Add straws and serve.

Spicy Banana Chill

A Caribbean combo to tantalize the taste buds with just a hint of heat in every mouthful of icy sweetness.

serves 2

1¼ cups milk	¾ cup banana ice cream
½ tsp mixed spice	2 bananas, sliced and frozen

Method

❶ Pour the milk into a food processor and add the mixed spice. Add half of the banana ice cream and process gently until combined, then add the remaining ice cream and process until well blended.

❷ When the mixture is well combined, add the frozen banana slices and process until smooth. Pour the mixture into tall glasses, add straws, and serve at once.

Cranberry Energizer

Top up your vitamin C levels—this is the perfect pick-me-up for getting going and waking up a sluggish system.

serves 2

1¼ cups cranberry juice

scant ½ cup orange juice

1 cup fresh raspberries

1 tbsp lemon juice

slices and spirals of fresh lemon or orange, to decorate

Method

❶ Pour the cranberry juice and orange juice into a food processor and process gently until combined. Add the raspberries and lemon juice and process until smooth.

❷ Pour the mixture into glasses and decorate with slices and spirals of fresh lemon or orange. Serve at once.

Caribbean Vegan Cocktail

Chill out with a tropical treat. If you close your eyes, you can almost hear the waves lapping on the beach.

serves 2

scant ½ cup coconut milk

scant 1 cup soy milk

scant ½ cup pineapple juice

1 tbsp brown sugar

1 ripe mango, pitted and diced

2 tbsp grated fresh coconut

1 cup frozen pineapple chunks

1 banana, sliced and frozen

To decorate

grated fresh coconut

wedges of fresh pineapple

Method

❶ Put the coconut milk, soy milk, pineapple juice, and sugar into a food processor and process gently until combined. Add the diced mango to the food processor along with the grated coconut and process well.

❷ Add the frozen pineapple chunks and banana slices and process until smooth. Pour the mixture into glasses, scatter over some grated fresh coconut, and decorate the rims with wedges of fresh pineapple. Serve at once.

Pineapple Soda

Ice cream soda for grown-ups, this luscious mix of pineapple, coconut milk, and vanilla ice cream is irresistible.

serves 2

¾ cup pineapple juice

scant ½ cup coconut milk

1 cup vanilla ice cream

1 cup frozen pineapple chunks

¾ cup sparkling water

2 scooped-out pineapple shells, to serve (optional)

Method

❶ Pour the pineapple juice and coconut milk into a food processor. Add the ice cream and process until smooth.

❷ Add the pineapple chunks and process well. Pour the mixture into scooped-out pineapple shells or tall glasses, until two-thirds full. Top up with sparkling water, add straws, and serve.

Pineapple & Coconut Shake

**The perfect partnership—and a lovely way to wind down at the end of a busy day
with your own perfect partner.**

serves 2

1½ cups pineapple juice

scant ½ cup coconut milk

¾ cup vanilla ice cream

1 cup frozen pineapple chunks

2 scooped-out coconut shells,
to serve (optional)

2 tbsp grated fresh coconut, to decorate

Method

❶ Pour the pineapple juice and coconut milk into a food processor. Add the ice cream and process until smooth.

❷ Add the pineapple chunks and process until smooth. Pour the mixture into scooped-out coconut shells or tall glasses, and decorate with grated fresh coconut. Add straws and serve.

Peach & Pineapple Smoothie

Sweet and creamy with a hint of sharpness, this elegant smoothie will appeal to sophisticated palates.

serves 2

½ cup pineapple juice

juice of 1 lemon

scant ½ cup water

3 tbsp brown sugar

¾ cup natural yogurt

1 peach, roughly chopped and frozen

¾ cup frozen pineapple chunks

wedges of fresh pineapple, to decorate

Method

❶ Pour the pineapple juice, lemon juice, and water into a food processor. Add the sugar and yogurt and process until blended.

❷ Add the frozen peach and pineapple chunks and process until smooth. Pour the mixture into glasses and decorate the rims with wedges of fresh pineapple.
Serve at once.

Pineapple Crush

A long, cool thirst quencher, this will boost your concentration and
revitalize a tired or stressed mind.

serves 2

scant ½ cup pineapple juice

4 tbsp orange juice

¾ cup melon, roughly chopped

1 cup frozen pineapple chunks

4 ice cubes

To decorate

slices of fresh melon

slices of fresh orange

Method

❶ Pour the pineapple juice and orange juice into a food processor and process gently until combined.

❷ Add the melon, pineapple, and ice cubes and process until a slushy consistency has been reached.

❸ Pour the mixture into glasses and decorate with slices of fresh melon and orange. Serve at once.

Hawaiian Shake

When your energy levels are flagging, give yourself a treat with this invigorating and exuberant shake.

serves 2

1 cup milk	To decorate
3½ tbsp coconut milk	grated fresh coconut
¾ cup vanilla ice cream	wedges of fresh pineapple
2 bananas, sliced and frozen	
1 cup canned pineapple chunks, drained	
1 papaya, seeded and diced	

Method

❶ Pour the milk and coconut milk into a food processor and process gently until combined. Add half of the ice cream and process gently, then add the remaining ice cream and process until smooth.

❷ Add the frozen banana slices and process well, then add the pineapple chunks and papaya and process until smooth. Pour the mixture into tall glasses, scatter over the grated coconut, and decorate the rims with pineapple wedges. Serve at once.

Pacific Smoothie

Luscious figs combine superbly with the nuts, orange juice, and maple syrup in this unusual and delicate drink.

serves 2

1½ cups hazelnut yogurt

2 tbsp freshly squeezed orange juice

4 tbsp maple syrup

8 large fresh figs, chopped

6 ice cubes

toasted chopped hazelnuts, to decorate

Method

❶ Pour the yogurt, orange juice, and maple syrup into a food processor and process gently until combined.

❷ Add the figs and ice cubes and process until smooth. Pour the mixture into glasses and scatter over some toasted chopped hazelnuts. Serve at once.

Rose Sunset

This beautifully fragrant drink, with its romantic name, has an equally delectable and illusive flavor.

serves 2

scant ½ cup natural yogurt

2 cups milk

1 tbsp rose water

3 tbsp honey

1 ripe mango, pitted and diced

6 ice cubes

edible rose petals, to decorate (optional)

Method

❶ Pour the yogurt and milk into a food processor and process gently until combined.

❷ Add the rose water and honey and process until thoroughly blended, then add the mango along with the ice cubes and process until smooth. Pour the mixture into glasses, decorate with edible rose petals, if using, and serve.

Fruit Rapture

Simple, but splendid, this restorative smoothie will get you back on track at any time of day.

serves 2

scant ½ cup milk

½ cup peach yogurt

scant ½ cup orange juice

8 oz/225 g canned peach slices, drained

6 ice cubes

strips of fresh orange peel, to decorate

Method

❶ Pour the milk, yogurt, and orange juice into a food processor and process gently until combined.

❷ Add the peach slices and ice cubes and process until smooth. Pour the mixture into glasses and decorate with strips of fresh orange peel. Add straws and serve.

Traditional Lemonade

A classic cooler that is redolent of a more leisured and peaceful era, this is a well-loved favorite.

serves 2

⅔ cup water	To decorate
6 tbsp sugar	wedge of lemon
1 tsp grated lemon rind	sugar
½ cup lemon juice	slices of fresh lemon
6 ice cubes	
sparkling water	

Method

❶ Put the water, sugar, and grated lemon rind into a small pan and bring to a boil, stirring constantly. Continue to boil, stirring, for 5 minutes.

❷ Remove from the heat and leave to cool to room temperature (about 30 minutes). Stir in the lemon juice, then transfer to a pitcher, cover with plastic wrap, and chill in the refrigerator for at least 2 hours.

❸ When the lemon mixture has almost finished chilling, take two glasses and rub the rims with a wedge of lemon, then dip them in sugar to frost. Put the ice cubes into the glasses.

❹ Remove the lemon mixture from the refrigerator, pour it over the ice, and top up with sparkling water. The ratio should be one part lemon mixture to three parts sparkling water. Stir well to mix, decorate with slices of fresh lemon, and serve.

Kiwi Dream

More than a whole day's dose of vitamin C in a glass, as well as a wonderfully refreshing sweet and sharp flavor.

serves 2

⅔ cup milk

juice of 2 limes

2 kiwi fruit, peeled and chopped

1 tbsp sugar

2 cups vanilla ice cream

To decorate

slices of fresh kiwi fruit

strips of fresh lime peel

Method

❶ Pour the milk and lime juice into a food processor and process gently until combined.

❷ Add the kiwi fruit and sugar and process gently, then add the ice cream and process until smooth. Pour the mixture into glasses and decorate with slices of fresh kiwi fruit and strips of fresh lime peel. Serve at once.

Banana & Apple Booster

Kick-start your day and wake up your taste buds with this zingy vitamin- and mineral-packed energizer.

serves 2

1 cup apple juice

½ tsp ground cinnamon

2 tsp grated fresh root ginger

2 bananas, sliced and frozen

slices of fresh banana on cocktail sticks,
to decorate

Method

❶ Pour the apple juice into a food processor. Add the cinnamon and ginger and process gently until combined.

❷ Add the frozen banana slices and process until smooth. Pour the mixture into tall glasses and decorate with slices of fresh banana on cocktail sticks. Serve at once.

Banana & Blueberry Smoothie

Sweet, sharp, fragrant, rich, and creamy, this is pure magic in a glass that will lift your spirits.

serves 2

¾ cup apple juice

½ cup natural yogurt

1 banana, sliced and frozen

1 cup frozen blueberries

whole fresh blueberries, to decorate

Method

❶ Pour the apple juice into a food processor. Add the yogurt and process until smooth.

❷ Add the frozen banana slices and half of the blueberries and process well, then add the remaining blueberries and process until smooth. Pour the mixture into tall glasses and decorate with whole fresh blueberries. Add straws and serve.

Raspberry Cooler

Liquid sunshine—not only is this superbly refreshing, but it also tones the whole system.

serves 2

8 ice cubes, crushed

2 tbsp raspberry syrup

2 cups chilled apple juice

whole fresh raspberries and pieces of apple on cocktail sticks, to decorate

Method

❶ Divide the crushed ice between two glasses. Pour the raspberry syrup over the ice.

❷ Top up each glass with chilled apple juice and stir well. Decorate with the whole fresh raspberries and pieces of apple on cocktail sticks and serve.

Berry Cream

The inspired combination of sweet banana and tart summer berries could almost be described as intoxicating.

serves 2

1½ cups orange juice

1 lb/450 g frozen berries
(such as blueberries, raspberries,
and blackberries)

1 banana, sliced and frozen

slices of fresh strawberry, to decorate

Method

❶ Pour the orange juice into a food processor. Add half of the frozen berries and the banana slices and process until smooth.

❷ Add the remaining berries and process until smooth. Pour the mixture into tall glasses and decorate the rims with slices of fresh strawberry. Add straws and serve.

Strawberry & Orange Smoothie

Probably one of the first smoothies ever invented, this impeccable combination remains a firm favorite.

serves 2

½ cup natural yogurt

¾ cup strawberry yogurt

¾ cup orange juice

generous ½ cup frozen sliced strawberries

1 banana, sliced and frozen

To decorate

slices of fresh orange

whole fresh strawberries

Method

❶ Pour the natural and strawberry yogurts into a food processor and process gently. Add the orange juice and process until the mixture is combined.

❷ Add the frozen strawberries and banana slices and process until smooth. Pour the mixture into tall glasses and decorate with slices of fresh orange and whole fresh strawberries. Add straws and serve.

Strawberry & Peach Smoothie

**One luscious glassful of this marvelously fruity mix and
you will feel restored, revived, and refreshed.**

serves 2

¾ cup milk

8 oz/225 g canned peach slices, drained

2 fresh apricots, chopped

12–14 fresh strawberries,
hulled and sliced

2 bananas, sliced and frozen

slices of fresh strawberries, to decorate

Method

❶ Pour the milk into a food processor. Add the peach slices and process gently until combined. Add the apricots and process gently until combined.

❷ Add the strawberries and banana slices and process until smooth. Pour the mixture into glasses and decorate the rims with fresh strawberries. Serve at once.

Summer & Citrus Fruit Punch

Serve this vibrant punch whenever you have something to celebrate, or just to make yourself feel good.

serves 2

4 tbsp orange juice	4 ice cubes
1 tbsp lime juice	whole fresh raspberries, black currants or
scant ½ cup sparkling water	blueberries, and blackberries on cocktail
2 cups frozen summer fruits	sticks, to decorate
(such as blueberries, raspberries,	
blackberries, and strawberries)	

Method

❶ Pour the orange juice, lime juice, and sparkling water into a food processor and process gently until combined.

❷ Add the frozen summer fruits and ice cubes and process until a slushy consistency has been reached.

❸ Pour the mixture into glasses, decorate with whole fresh raspberries, black currants or blueberries, and blackberries on cocktail sticks, and serve.

Cherry Kiss

This long and lively cooler is a welcome way to turn off the heat
in the middle of summer.

serves 2

8 ice cubes, crushed

2 tbsp cherry syrup

2 cups sparkling water

maraschino cherries on cocktail sticks,
to decorate

Method

❶ Divide the crushed ice between two glasses and pour over the cherry syrup.

❷ Top up each glass with sparkling water. Decorate with the maraschino cherries on cocktail sticks and serve.

Vegetables & Spices

Red Bell Pepper Reactor

Boost your energy levels and fire up your system with this truly dynamic vegetable medley.

serves 2

1 cup carrot juice

1 cup tomato juice

2 large red bell peppers,
seeded and roughly chopped

1 tbsp lemon juice

pepper

Method

❶ Pour the carrot juice and tomato juice into a food processor and process gently until combined.

❷ Add the bell peppers and lemon juice. Season with plenty of freshly ground black pepper and process until smooth. Pour the mixture into tall glasses, add straws, and serve.

Ginger Crush

The sweet, mild flavors of carrot and tomato are literally gingered up
in this enlivening drink.

serves 2

1 cup carrot juice

4 tomatoes, skinned, seeded, and
roughly chopped

1 tbsp lemon juice

½ cup roughly chopped fresh parsley

1 tbsp grated fresh root ginger

6 ice cubes

½ cup water

chopped fresh parsley, to garnish

Method

❶ Put the carrot juice, tomatoes, and lemon juice into a food processor and process gently until combined.

❷ Add the parsley to the food processor along with the ginger and ice cubes.

Process until well combined, then pour in the water and process until smooth.

❸ Pour the mixture into tall glasses and garnish with chopped fresh parsley. Serve at once.

Peppermint Ice

Simultaneously hot and cold on the tongue, this classic combination still manages to surprise.

serves 2

⅔ cup milk

2 tbsp peppermint syrup

2 cups peppermint ice cream

sprigs of fresh mint, to decorate

Method

❶ Pour the milk and peppermint syrup into a food processor and process gently until combined.

❷ Add the peppermint ice cream and process until smooth. Pour the mixture into tall glasses and decorate with sprigs of fresh mint. Add straws and serve.

Cinnamon & Lemon Tea

Enjoy this aromatic winter warmer and, at the same time, keep the worst of the weather and colds at bay.

serves 2

1¾ cups water

4 cloves

1 small stick of cinnamon

2 tea bags

3–4 tbsp lemon juice

1–2 tbsp brown sugar

slices of fresh lemon, to decorate

Method

❶ Put the water, cloves, and cinnamon into a pan and bring to a boil. Remove from the heat and add the tea bags. Leave to infuse for 5 minutes, then remove the tea bags.

❷ Stir in lemon juice and sugar to taste. Return the pan to low heat and warm through gently. Do not boil.

❸ Remove the pan from the heat and strain the tea into heatproof glasses. Decorate with slices of fresh lemon and serve.

Celery Surprise

A savory delight that not only acts as a tonic, but also cleanses and refreshes the palate.

serves 2

½ cup carrot juice

1 lb/450 g tomatoes, skinned, seeded, and roughly chopped

1 tbsp lemon juice

4 celery stalks, trimmed and sliced

4 scallions, trimmed and roughly chopped

½ cup roughly chopped fresh parsley

1 well-packed cup fresh mint

2 celery stalks, to garnish

Method

❶ Put the carrot juice, tomatoes, and lemon juice into a food processor and process gently until combined.

❷ Add the sliced celery along with the scallions, parsley, and mint and process until smooth. Pour the mixture into tall glasses and garnish with celery stalks. Serve at once.

Curried Crush

Juice with attitude—this stimulating blend of flavors is guaranteed to
add spice to your life.

serves 2

1 cup carrot juice	1 garlic clove, chopped
4 tomatoes, skinned, seeded, and roughly chopped	½ cup roughly chopped fresh parsley
1 tbsp lemon juice	1 tsp curry powder
2 celery stalks, trimmed and sliced	6 ice cubes
1 small romaine lettuce	½ cup water
	2 celery stalks, to garnish

Method

❶ Put the carrot juice, tomatoes, lemon juice, and celery into a food processor and process gently until combined.

❷ Separate the lettuce leaves, then wash them and add them to the food processor along with the garlic, parsley, curry powder, and ice cubes. Process until well combined, then pour in the water and process until smooth.

❸ Pour the mixture into tall glasses and garnish with celery stalks. Serve at once.

Watercress Float

Peppery watercress perks up carrot juice and provides extra vitamins and minerals in this cleansing drink. If watercress is unavailable, use arugula instead.

serves 2

2 cups carrot juice

½ cup watercress or arugula leaves

1 tbsp lemon juice

sprigs of fresh watercress or arugula, to garnish

Method

❶ Pour the carrot juice into a food processor. Add the watercress and lemon juice and process until smooth. Transfer to a pitcher, cover with plastic wrap, and chill in the refrigerator for at least 1 hour, or until required.

❷ When the mixture is thoroughly chilled, pour into glasses and garnish with sprigs of fresh watercress. Serve at once.

Orange & Carrot Smoothie

This doesn't just taste and look fabulous, but contains abundant, health-giving beta-carotene and vitamin C.

serves 2

¾ cup carrot juice

¾ cup orange juice

¾ cup vanilla ice cream

6 ice cubes

To decorate

slices of fresh orange

strips of fresh orange peel

Method

❶ Pour the carrot juice and orange juice into a food processor and process gently until well combined. Add the ice cream and process until thoroughly blended.

❷ Add the ice cubes and process until smooth. Pour the mixture into glasses, decorate with slices of fresh orange and strips of fresh orange peel, and serve.

Red Storm

A sure-fire lip-smacker, this spicy little number is definitely not for the unwary or faint-hearted.

serves 2

2 cups tomato juice

dash of Worcestershire sauce

1 small red chile,
seeded and chopped

1 scallion, trimmed and chopped

6 ice cubes

2 long, thin red chiles, cut into flowers
(see method), to garnish

Method

❶ To make the chile flowers, use a sharp knife to make six cuts along each chile. Place the point of the knife about ½ inch/ 1 cm from the stalk end and cut toward the tip. Put the chiles in a bowl of iced water and leave them for 25–30 minutes, until they have spread out into flower shapes.

❷ Put the tomato juice and Worcestershire sauce into a food processor and process gently until combined. Add the chopped chile, scallion, and ice cubes and process until smooth.

❸ Pour the mixture into glasses and garnish with the chile flowers. Add straws and serve.

Sweets
& Coffees

Rich Chocolate Shake

The ultimate milkshake for children and chocoholics of all ages, this is supremely satisfying.

serves 2

⅔ cup milk

2 tbsp chocolate syrup

2 cups chocolate ice cream

grated chocolate, to decorate

Method

❶ Pour the milk and chocolate syrup into a food processor and process gently until combined.

❷ Add the chocolate ice cream and process until smooth. Pour the mixture into tall glasses and decorate by floating the grated chocolate. Serve at once.

Maple & Almond Milkshake

Go on. Why not indulge your sweet tooth with this rather grown-up, rich-tasting, novel milkshake?

serves 2

⅔ cup milk

2 tbsp maple syrup

2 cups vanilla ice cream

1 tbsp almond essence

chopped almonds, to decorate

Method

❶ Pour the milk and maple syrup into a food processor and process gently until combined.

❷ Add the ice cream and almond essence and process until smooth. Pour the mixture into glasses and decorate with the chopped almonds. Add straws and serve.

Coffee Whip

The magical pairing of coffee and chocolate can only be improved with the
addition of whipped cream.

serves 2

¾ cups milk

3½ tbsp light cream

1 tbsp brown sugar

2 tbsp cocoa powder

1 tbsp coffee syrup or
instant coffee powder

6 ice cubes

To serve

whipped cream

grated chocolate

Method

❶ Put the milk, cream, and sugar into a food processor and process gently until combined.

❷ Add the cocoa powder and coffee syrup or powder and process well, then add the ice cubes and process until smooth.

❸ Pour the mixture into glasses. Top with whipped cream, scatter over the grated chocolate, and serve.

Banana & Coffee Milkshake

A powerhouse drink for those who lead life on the run, this unusual milkshake tastes great, too.

serves 2

1¼ cups milk

4 tbsp instant coffee powder

¾ cup vanilla ice cream

2 bananas, sliced and frozen

Method

❶ Pour the milk into a food processor, add the coffee powder, and process gently until combined. Add half of the vanilla ice cream and process gently, then add the remaining ice cream and process until well combined.

❷ When the mixture is thoroughly blended, add the frozen banana slices and process until smooth. Pour the mixture into glasses and serve.

Smooth Iced Coffee

Nothing could be nicer after a long, lazy, alfresco lunch than this cool, elegant iced coffee.

serves 2

1¾ cups water

2 tbsp instant coffee crystals

2 tbsp brown sugar

6 ice cubes

To decorate

light cream

whole coffee beans

Method

❶ Use the water and coffee crystals to brew some hot coffee, then leave to cool to room temperature (about 30 minutes). Transfer to a pitcher, cover with plastic wrap, and chill in the refrigerator for at least 45 minutes.

❷ When the coffee has chilled, pour it into a food processor. Add the sugar and process until well combined. Add the ice cubes and process until smooth.

❸ Pour the mixture into glasses. Float light cream on the top, decorate with whole coffee beans, and serve.

Hazelnut & Coffee Sparkle

Try something a little different—you will be pleasantly surprised by how successful this mix is.

serves 2

1 cup water	To decorate
3 tbsp instant coffee crystals	slices of fresh lime
½ cup sparkling water	slices of fresh lemon
1 tbsp hazelnut syrup	
2 tbsp brown sugar	
6 ice cubes	

Method

❶ Use the water and coffee crystals to brew some hot coffee, then leave to cool to room temperature (about 30 minutes). Transfer to a pitcher, cover with plastic wrap, and chill in the refrigerator for at least 45 minutes.

❷ When the coffee has chilled, pour it into a food processor. Add the sparkling water, hazelnut syrup, and sugar, and process well. Add the ice cubes and process until smooth.

❸ Pour the mixture into glasses, decorate the rims with slices of fresh lime and lemon, and serve.

Peppermint Mocha

This exhilarating fusion of flavors could certainly set tongues wagging—
but only with sheer delight.

serves 2

1¾ cups milk

¾ cup coffee syrup

scant ½ cup peppermint syrup

1 tbsp chopped fresh mint leaves

4 ice cubes

To decorate

grated chocolate

sprigs of fresh mint

Method

❶ Pour the milk, coffee syrup, and peppermint syrup into a food processor and process gently until combined.

❷ Add the mint and ice cubes and process until a slushy consistency has been reached.

❸ Pour the mixture into glasses. Scatter over the grated chocolate, decorate with sprigs of fresh mint, and serve.

Drinks List

- Banana & Apple Booster *44* • Banana & Blueberry Smoothie *46*

- Banana & Coffee Milkshake *88* • Berry Cream *50* • Caribbean Vegan Cocktail *22*

- Celery Surprise *70* • Cherry Kiss *58* • Cinnamon & Lemon Tea *68* • Coffee Whip *86*

- Cranberry Energizer *20* • Curried Crush *72* • Fruit Cooler *16* • Fruit Rapture *38*

- Ginger Crush *64* • Hawaiian Shake *32* • Hazelnut & Coffee Sparkle *92*

- Kiwi Dream *42* • Maple & Almond Milkshake *84* • Melon Medley *10*

- Nectarine Melt *12* • Orange & Carrot Smoothie *76* • Orange & Lime Iced Tea *14*

- Pacific Smoothie *34* • Peach & Pineapple Smoothie *28* • Peppermint Ice *66*

- Peppermint Mocha *94* • Pineapple & Coconut Shake *26* • Pineapple Crush *30*

- Pineapple Soda *24* • Raspberry Cooler *48* • Red Bell Pepper Reactor *62*

- Red Storm *78* • Rich Chocolate Shake *82* • Rose Sunset *36* • Smooth Iced Coffee *90*

- Spicy Banana Chill *18* • Strawberry & Orange Smoothie *52*

- Strawberry & Peach Smoothie *54* • Summer & Citrus Fruit Punch *56*

- Traditional Lemonade *40* • Watercress Float *74*